# A KID'S ACTIVITY BOOK ON
# MONEY AND
# FINANCE

## TEACH CHILDREN ABOUT SAVING, BORROWING, AND PLANNING FOR THE FUTURE

Allan Kunigis

ILLUSTRATED BY
John Kurtz

FOR
YOUNG
READERS

T0019231

# TABLE OF CONTENTS

# DEAR PARENTS,

Welcome to *A Kid's Activity Book on Money and Finance.*

This book is intended as a fun, engaging introduction to money for young school-age children.

As you are surely aware, financial literacy is a serious issue in our society. As children begin to learn the basics of reading, writing, and arithmetic, it is the perfect time to start them off on the right path toward financial responsibility.

This book contains a variety of activities relating to money, and earning, saving, spending, and sharing it. To keep the content light, fun, and age appropriate, we've included some poems and rhyming messages here and there.

Overall, I believe there is a good mix of fun and engaging activities, which should provide an enjoyable and educational experience for your child. In some cases, you might help your children through an activity if they are challenged by it.

And what a great way to begin an ongoing dialogue with them about the basics of money management! That parent-child discussion will surely evolve and deepen as they gradually are able to grasp more about financial responsibility in the coming years.

I wish you and your child plenty of fun as you help them and encourage them to learn about the basics of money and money management through this activity book. I hope it lays the groundwork for a life of personal financial awareness and success.

# CHAPTER 1:
# WHAT IS MONEY?

## Introduction:

This is a fun activity book about money. In it, you will learn how to count money, use it, save it, spend it, earn it, and share it. Our aim is to help young people learn about money and have fun.

Maybe you got some money as a present. Do you receive an allowance? What do you use your money for? You could buy candy or snacks. Or buy a toy, or maybe save up for a bicycle or scooter.

Money is a way to pay for things that we buy. We can use coins. Each penny is worth 1 cent (1¢). A nickel is worth 5 cents (5¢). A dime is worth 10 cents (10¢). A quarter is worth 25 cents (25¢). We can also use paper money, like a one-dollar ($1) bill, or a five-dollar ($5) or a ten-dollar ($10) bill.

A long time ago, people didn't have money. They hunted and farmed for their food. If they needed other things, they traded with each other. You could bake bread and trade that for berries or apples. Or trade a cow for wood. You can't EAT a house! You need to HEAT it!

To make things easier, people started using metals. They used bronze, copper, silver, and gold. And then paper money was invented. That made it even easier! Today, we can buy things without coins and paper money. We can write checks, use credit cards, debit cards, or digital money.

Let's look at coins and paper money. See if you can name coins and their values and solve the crossword puzzle in the next few pages.

## How Much Are These Coins Worth?

Show the value of these coins:

**What is this coin?**

**What is its value?**
**(How many cents is it?)**

_____          _____

**Can you name
this coin?**

**What is its value?**

_____          _____

## What is this coin?          What is it worth?

_____          _____

## What is this coin?          What is it worth?

_____          _____

Answers on page 74.

# Coin Matching Game

Match the name of the money unit (coin or bill) with its value on the right. Draw a line to join each matching pair.

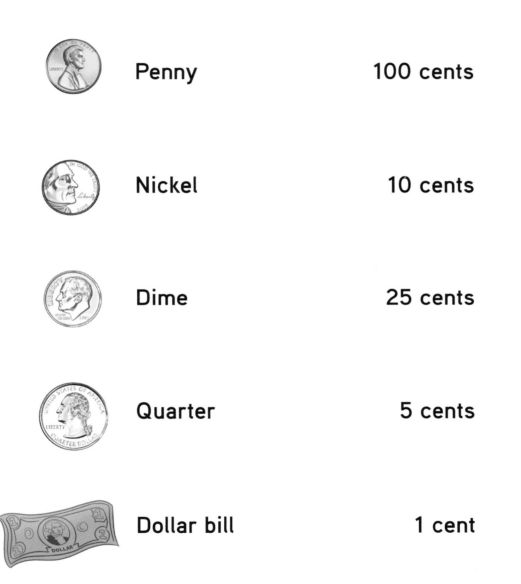

| | |
|---|---|
| Penny | 100 cents |
| Nickel | 10 cents |
| Dime | 25 cents |
| Quarter | 5 cents |
| Dollar bill | 1 cent |

Answers on page 74.

# MONEY CROSSWORD PUZZLE

## Clues:

**ACROSS**

2. Start of "century."

3. Lowest value of paper money.

5. Metallic object we use to buy

    things.

6. Another word for gift.

8. The focus of this book.

    (It rhymes with "honey.")

**DOWN**

1. Four of these = one dollar.

3. It's worth 10 cents.

4. Opposite of OFF.

6. It's worth one cent.

7. Five of these = 25 cents.

# CHAPTER 2:
# COUNTING MONEY

## Want to Count With Money?

With pennies, we count one by one.

Nickels are worth five
Like your fingers and thumb.

Dimes are worth ten
Like a nickel and a nickel again.

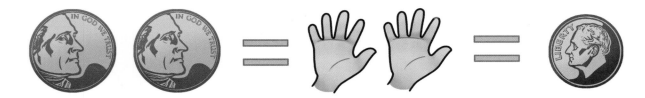

Can you count coins to twenty-five?
It's easy if you go by five.
Just like five pennies make a nickel
Five nickels equal one quarter.

If you think of fives
Your counting comes alive!

So, how many pennies can Jenny take
To make a quarter for an even break?
Did you say 25 (twenty-five)?
Hurray, we have arrived!

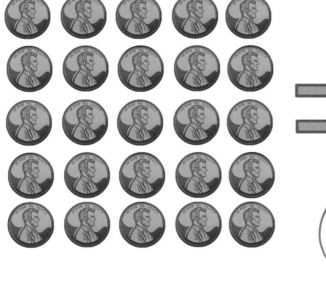

Have Some FUN
with MONEY!

# Money Rhymes
(Warning: Silliness Ahead!)

Jenny had a penny
And gave it to Benny
But then, Jenny didn't have any!
And Benny had MANY!

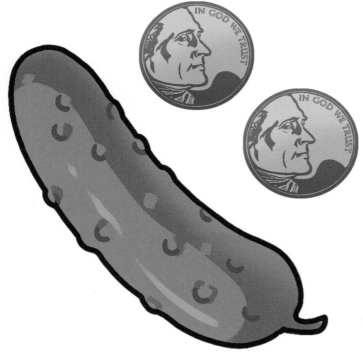

Dick L. had a nickel
But he couldn't buy a pickle
Because a pickle cost a dime.
How many nickels would Dick L. need
To buy himself a pickle to eat?
Did you say "two"!?
That's right! YAHOO!

If carrots cost a quarter
And you had one dollar
How many would you order?
And would they make you grow taller!?

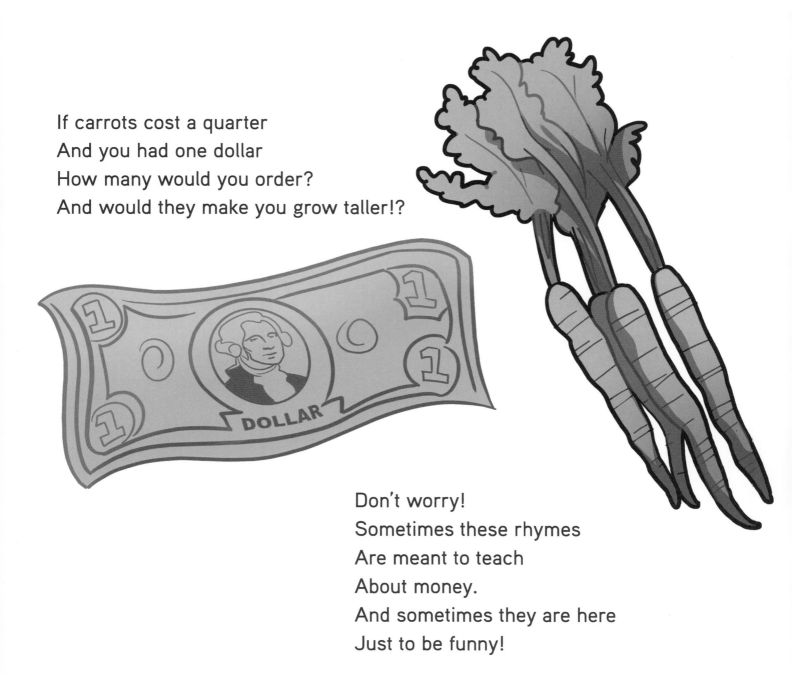

Don't worry!
Sometimes these rhymes
Are meant to teach
About money.
And sometimes they are here
Just to be funny!

# CAN YOU ANSWER THESE COIN QUESTIONS?

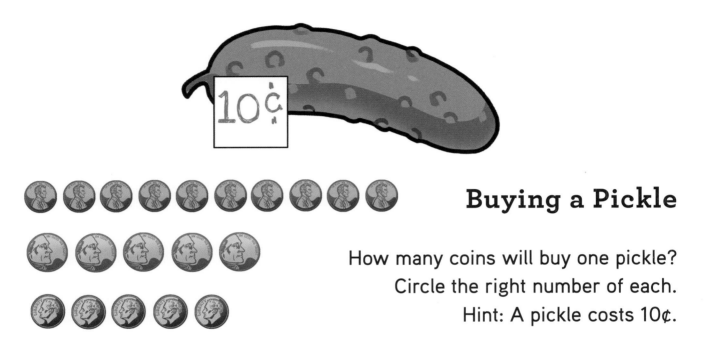

## Buying a Pickle

How many coins will buy one pickle?
Circle the right number of each.
Hint: A pickle costs 10¢.

Answer: _____

## Feeding Your Bunny

Buy carrots to feed your bunny.
If carrots cost 25¢ each and
you have 4 quarters, how many
carrots can you buy for your bunny?

Answer: _____

Answers on page 74.

# COINS AND BILLS

Paper bills are worth more than shiny coins. Do you know how many quarters equal a $1 bill?

Hint: Picture a pizza with four slices!

Did you say four?

Correct. Let's do some more!

How many dimes are equal to a $1 bill?
Hint: As many pennies are equal to a dime!

Did you say ten?

You are correct again!

# Shopping for School Supplies

What coins would you use to buy these school supplies?

## Eraser

An eraser costs 10 cents (10¢).

How many dimes would you need to buy it?_____

How many nickels?_____

How many pennies?_____

If you paid with a quarter, how
much change would you get back?_____

Answers on page 74.

# Composition Notebook

A notebook costs 49¢.
How many of each coin would you need to buy it, combining coins to pay the exact amount?

Quarters:_____

Dimes:_____

Nickels:_____

Pennies:_____

If you paid with a $1 bill, how
much change would you get back?_____

Answers on page 74.

# Box of 24 Crayons

A box of crayons costs 97¢.
How many of each coin would you need to buy it?

Quarters:_____

Dimes:_____

Nickels:_____

Pennies:_____

If you paid with $1, how
much change would you get back?_____

Answers on page 74.

# COIN MAZE

Can you find your way out? Go from the START in the middle to the FINISH by landing on dimes. Follow squares next to each other and don't land on any nickels or pennies.

# CHAPTER 3:
# EARNING MONEY

Extra chores

Bake sale

## How Can You Earn Money?

Where do you get money? Children can receive money as presents or get an allowance. You can also earn money by doing, making, or selling things.

Have you ever earned money? Have you wondered how you could? Let's list some things you could do.

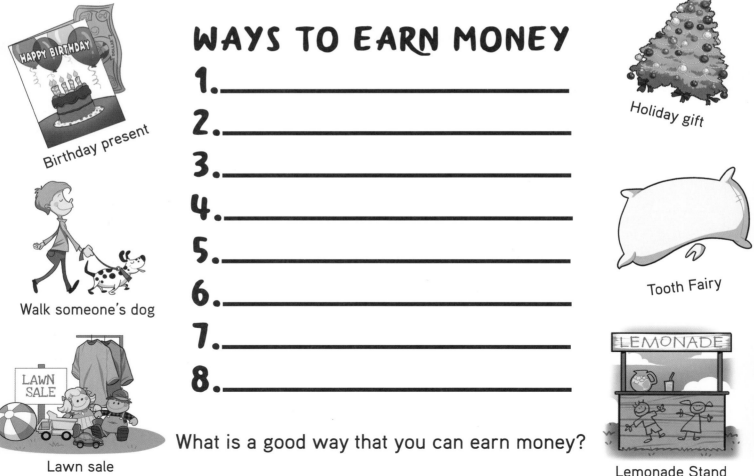

Birthday present

Walk someone's dog

Lawn sale

# WAYS TO EARN MONEY
1._____
2._____
3._____
4._____
5._____
6._____
7._____
8._____

Holiday gift

Tooth Fairy

Lemonade Stand

What is a good way that you can earn money?

# CONNECT THE DOTS

## Have You Ever Set Up Your Own Business?

What could you do with lemons, water, sugar and ice cubes? You and a friend could sell this on a hot day. Remember, you'll need a table, sign, pitcher, and glasses. Connect the dots and see.

Answers on page 75.

# EARNING MONEY CROSSWORD PUZZLE

## Clues:

### Across

2. You can do this with money you earn and don't save. (Hint: Rhymes with END)

3. Do your parents give you an _ _ _ _ _ _ _ _ _ to spend, save, or share?

5. You can _ _ _ _ money you earn but don't spend. (Rhymes with WAVE)

8. Do you earn money by doing extra _ _ _ _ _ _ around the house? (Rhymes with BORES)

9. Money you get on your birthday is a _ _ _ _.

10. Opposite of go slow. (Rhymes with BLURRY)

### Down

1. Tommy likes to _ _ _ _ _ his money with others.

2. You can sell your old toys and books at lawn _ _ _ _ _.

4. Your parents' car is dirty. Maybe you could earn money if you _ _ _ _ _ it. (Rhymes with MEAN)

6. When someone has a job, he or she _ _ _ _ _ money.

7. Put this under your pillow to get money from a fairy.

Answers on page 75.

# EARNING MONEY AT A BAKE SALE

Have you ever held a bake sale? You can earn money by baking yummy food!

Lucas, Sophia, and Emily earned some money by doing a bake sale. How much did they earn?

Lucas baked 12 chocolate chip cookies and he charged 50¢ for each one. He sold all 12 cookies. How much did Lucas earn?

$_____

Sophia baked 12 apple muffins. She charged $1 each. She sold 10 muffins. How much did Sophia earn?

$_____

Emily baked 12 chocolate brownies. She charged $1 each and she sold them all. How much did Emily earn?

$_____

Now, add up how much they all earned:

$ _____ + $ _____ + $ _____ = $ _____.

Answers on page 76.

# CHAPTER 4:
# USING MONEY

## Goldilocks and the Three Jars

Once upon a time, a little girl named Goldilocks went for a walk in the woods. She saw a house and knocked on the door. When no one answered, she walked in.

On a shelf, she saw three jars of money. She wondered what they were. She looked closely and saw three signs: Saving, Spending, and Sharing.

Just then, she heard a sound! She turned around and saw three bears. They were just as surprised to see her as little Goldilocks was to see them.

Instead of running away, Goldilocks asked the three bears about their jars. They were happy to explain:

"The spending jar is for things we need right away," said Mama bear. "Things like milk, honey, and porridge."
"The saving jar is for things that cost more money," explained Papa bear. "Those are things we need to save up for. Maybe a new bed when the old one gets too lumpy, or a new chair if one is broken!" And he winked at Goldilocks with a playful look.

"The sharing jar is for sharing with others," Baby bear piped in with excitement. "We like sharing! Would you like to stay and share dinner with us? Momma and poppa, can she!?"

They nodded yes. Goldilocks thought for a second, and said, "Yes, that would be so nice!"

And she stayed and made friends with the three bears. She was so thankful that they taught her about the three jars and she made three new friends.

# WHAT WOULD YOU DO WITH MONEY?

What can you do with money that you have earned or were given? Here are three common choices. You could:

1. Spend it.
2. Share it with others.
3. Save it up for something special and watch it grow!

Let's look at the fun things we can use money for.

## Money Jumble

See if you can unjumble the letters to solve these word puzzles.

1. If something doesn't cost money it is _ _ _ _. (Rhymes with "me")

    R E F E

2. A place where you deposit and save
    money is a _ _ _ _.

    N K A B

3. These shiny metals are really old.
    They are made of silver and _ _ _ _.

    O D L G

4. I bought food for our next meal. I paid less because I got a good _ _ _ _!

A D L E

5. I paid half price for this hammer and nail.
That's because they were on _ _ _ _.

A L E S

6. When you don't spend money, you can
_ _ _ _ it.

A S V E

7. When you put money in a bank, it can earn more _ _ _ _ _.

Y O N E M

8. If you get an allowance, you can
save it, spend it, or _ _ _ _ _ it.

H E A R S

Answers on page 76.

# IT'S TIME FOR MONEY RHYMES!

Look for words with CAPITAL letters. The answers will rhyme with them!

BRAVE DAVE hid in a CAVE. His friend WAVED and asked to borrow some money. Because DAVE GAVE, he had no money left to _ _ _ _ for himself.

CLAIRE went to the FAIR WHERE she won a Teddy BEAR. Her friend was sad because she didn't win one too. So, CLAIRE decided to _ _ _ _ _ her BEAR.

Jen's FRIEND Jim asked her to LEND him some money. Although Jen had less money to _ _ _ _ on herself, she was happy to SEND some to a FRIEND.

ROY was full of JOY like any BOY with a new _ _ _.
(Hint: Something you can buy and play with.)

Roy's friend BENNY didn't have ANY but he had a shine new _ _ _ _ _.
(Hint: It's a coin worth one cent.)

So Benny HOPPED, FLOPPED, and BOPPED to the _ _ _ _.
(Hint: Another name for store.)

Answers on page 76.

# Three Jars

Three jars sat
On a shelf in my room
At first they were empty
Until I heard this tune.

In the first jar you put
Money to save.
It might seem easy
Until you crave
Something to buy
And then you learn why.
It can be good to wait
And save up for something great!

In the second jar you have
Money to spend.
If that jar were full
It would never end.
But that's not the case
So let's not waste
The money we use
With no excuse.

In the third jar we place
Money to share.
We do that because
It's nice to care.

Some people don't have
As much as us.
So no need to argue,
Scream or fuss.
Just give some to feed
Those with a need.

There they are:
Three jars on a shelf.
Each with a role
Like Santa's elf.

Think about putting
Something in each.
It's a simple thing
To learn or to teach.

Save-Spend-Share
Because you care.
Share-Save-Spend
It's what we intend.
Spend-Share-Save
You don't need to be brave!
Just put something in each.
It's within your reach!

# SHOW ME THE MONEY WORD SEARCH

Can you find the MONEY words in this Word Search puzzle? They could go across, down or on a diagonal.

```
T M K C A N D Y D
T A H P A Y B G Z
S Q T O Y S C I M
S A V E P Z H F O
P H P E N N Y T N
E C O I N S W S E
N L C P G W P E Y
D B A N K G X L J
C H A N G E Y L X
```

CHANGE    COINS    PENNY    SHOP    GIFT
MONEY     CANDY    SELL     CASH    PAY
SPEND     PIGGY    BANK     SAVE    TOY

Answers on page 76.

# CHAPTER 5:
# SAVING MONEY

## Save Your Money: It's Easy and Fun!

I wanted to save some money
So I put it in a drawer.
But when I opened the drawer
The money was no more!

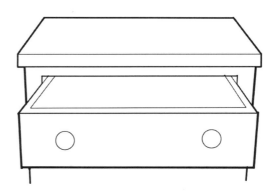

I put some coins in a jar
But the money didn't go far.

I placed some dimes in a piggy bank
But then I had no one else to thank!

Then I walked to the bank on the corner
To talk to the teller but no one had warned her!

I deposited some money
And she was surprised!
She acted kind of funny
And looked me in the eyes.

She opened an account for me
So I could save more money.
Maybe I'd get it from my parents
Or Santa, the Tooth Fairy, or an Easter Bunny!

I like going to the bank
So my money can grow and grow.
I'm not tempted to spend it
And I wanted you to know.

You can do
it, too.
It's really kind of fun.
The bank keeps it safe for you
And it can do it for anyone!

**Color the pictures that go with this poem.**

# FIND THE HIDDEN MESSAGES

Can You Solve This Secret Code?

## Can you crack the code to find the message?

Replace each letter under the blanks in the riddle with the one before it in the alphabet. If you see a "b," then the letter above it is an "a." We'll show the first one to start you off.

S _ _ _    _ _ _ _    _ _ _ _ _
T B W F    T P N F    N P O F Z

Answers on page 76.

## Unscramble the Letters

Unscramble the letters below each word. Then write the word on the letter blanks.

_ _ _ _    _ _ _ _ _    _ _ _    _ _ _ _    _ _ _ _ _.

NTDO    DEPNS    LAL    ROYU    YONEM

## Save up for something special.

Connect the dots to see what it is.

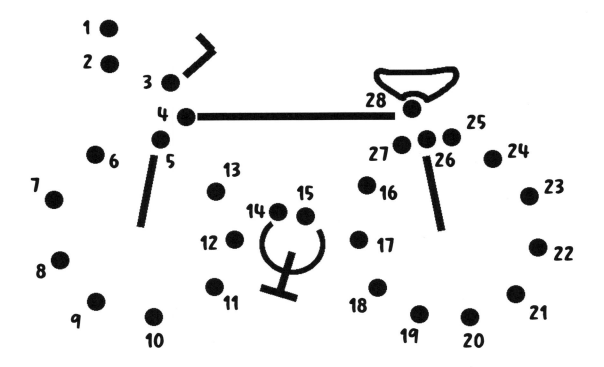

Answers on page 77.

# What Would You Save For?

Can you think of something special that you would save your money for? Draw a picture of it below:

# Now, answer these three questions:

1. How much does it cost?

2. How much money could you save each month?

3. How many months would it take to save enough to buy it?

Let's say you want to buy a wooden castle building block set. It costs $100. If you save $10 each month, how long would you have to save before you could buy it?

Write down your goal. Start saving for it now! And keep track of your saving.

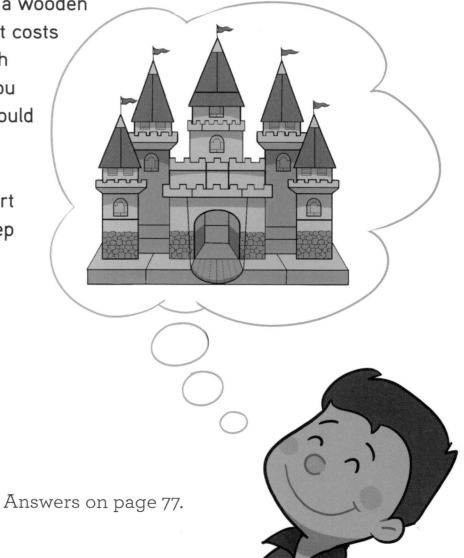

Answers on page 77.

# Solve the Missing Letters With a Secret Code!

This game uses a secret code. Every letter in the alphabet has a number. Replace the number with the right letter.

Use this to help crack the code:

| A | B | C | D | E | F | G | H | I | J |
|---|---|---|---|---|---|---|---|---|---|
| 1 | 2 | 3 | 4 | 5 | 6 | 7 | 8 | 9 | 10 |

| K | L | M | N | O | P | Q | R | S | T |
|---|---|---|---|---|---|---|---|---|---|
| 11 | 12 | 13 | 14 | 15 | 16 | 17 | 18 | 19 | 20 |

| U | V | W | X | Y | Z |
|---|---|---|---|---|---|
| 21 | 22 | 23 | 24 | 25 | 26 |

Now, let's solve the missing letters in these sentences:

Banks keep your money S _ _ _.
Code numbers:          19-1-6-5

In a bank, your money can earn _ _ T _ _ _ S _.
Code numbers:          9-14-20-5-18-5-19-20

Putting money in your bank account is a D _ P _ _ _ _
Code numbers:          4-5-16-15-19-9-20.

Answers on page 77.

# CHAPTER 6:
# SPENDING MONEY

## Spending Choices

Spending money can be fun. There are so many things you could buy. Make smart choices so you can buy more with your money!

## Big or small? Now or later?

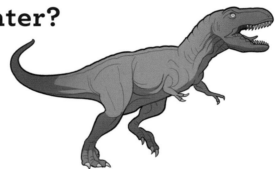

What can you buy for $1 or $2?

Here are some ideas:

Candy. A small toy, like a small plastic dinosaur. Fluffy slime. Play-Doh. A used toy or book. What else? List your ideas:

1._____

2._____

3._____

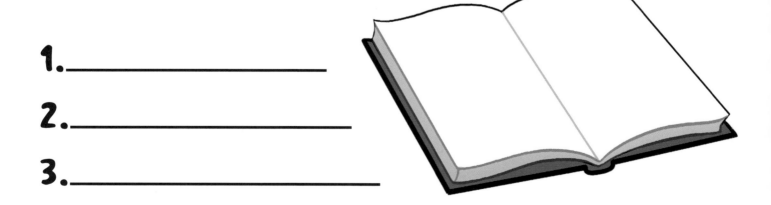

What you could buy for $10? Perhaps a better or nicer toy. A book. Clothes. A meal. What else?

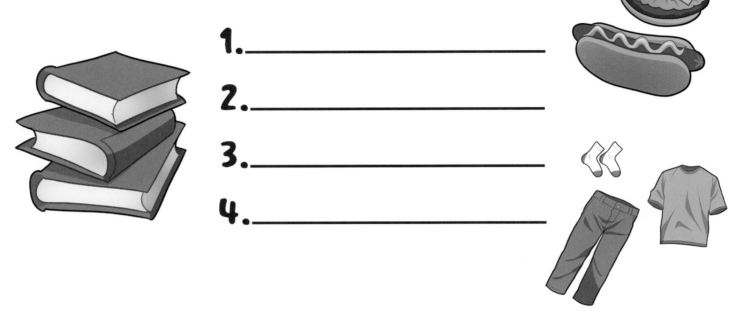

1._____

2._____

3._____

4._____

What could you buy for $50? Maybe a special toy, like a scooter, or a really pretty doll. Maybe a few meals or a special meal. What else? There are so many choices.

1._____

2._____

3._____

4._____

What choices would you make if you had $10?

There's no right or wrong answer. Here are a few choices:

A) Buy a few little toys or treats for $1 or $2 each.

B) Buy one thing for $10.

C) Save the money until you have $50 and then buy something bigger, better, or nicer.

Think about what you would buy. Can you draw a picture of it?

# SPENDING MONEY CROSSWORD PUZZLE

## Clues:

## Across

1. Good shoppers _ _ _ _ _ _ _ two or more products to see which is best.

3. I could borrow a _ _ _ _ from a library or buy it in a store. (Hint: Rhymes with LOOK)

4. When I am older, I want to buy a _ _ _ _ phone. (Rhymes with BELL)

5. I'm so hungry I could _ _ _ a huge meal!

9. I want to buy a _ _ _ _ _ _ _ to ride. (Rhymes with HOOTER)

11. I like playing video _ _ _ _ _.

12. What is your favorite _ _ _ _ _ _ _? Mine is ice cream!

## Down

1. Sometimes you have to _ _ _ _ _ _ between two things. (Rhymes with LOSE)

2. How much you pay for something: _ _ _ _ _. (Rhymes with RICE)

3. If someone sells you something, you _ _ _ it. (Rhymes with WHY)

6. I love playing with new _ _ _ _. (Rhymes with BOYS)

7. When my mom buys cereal, she buys the family_ _ _ _. (Rhymes with CRIES)

8. My friends and I like to play at the video _ _ _ _ _ _. (Rhymes with PARADE)

10. Ice cream is my favorite summer _ _ _ _ _.

Answers on page 78.

# MATCH THE COUPONS

Do you or your family ever clip coupons to save some money when you shop? Let's see if you can match the coupon on the left with the product on the right.

| | |
|---|---|
| "Buy 1 meal. Get the second meal free." Coupon for McFriendly's Restaurant |  |
| "Save $ on 2 LARGE boxes of Kooky Looky or Wakey Flakey Cereal" |  |
| "Buy 2 Pints of Happy Treats Ice Cream at half price" |  |
| "Save $3 on a SATURDAY movie at a Flicks-Plex Theater" |  |
| "Save 20% on a 6-pack of Yummy Tummy juice boxes" |  |

Answers on page 78.

# CHAPTER 7:
# SHARING MONEY

## Share Because You Care

Money can help you buy fun stuff
Like candy or toys.
You can also buy things
For other girls and boys!

Sharing with others can be lots of fun.
Do you know how you can get it done?
You could give money in person
To a neighbor or a friend.
Or send it in the mail or online
And just press "SEND"!

What is the opposite of "GREED"?
It's helping others who have a NEED.
And it feels nice to do a good deed!
How can money help other people? Let's see . . .

**Sally** doesn't have enough food to eat.
Maybe she could use some money
To buy vegetables or meat!
And perhaps she could also have a special treat!

**Gina** needs safe water to drink.
The water from her tap kind of looks like ink
And boy, it tastes funny and it REALLY stinks!
But if her family had some money
They might do something cool
They could dig a well or buy bottled water at school.

**Mario** doesn't have books to read.
So how can you help solve his need?
Let's take a closer look:
By giving money so his parents can buy a book!

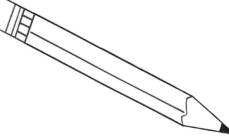

There are so many ways to share
And once you're aware
You can see needs everywhere!
Of course, there's only so much you can do
But every bit counts, from me and from you!

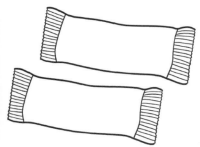
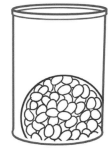

## How can you help others?

Giving money is one way to share.
What are other ways?

1._____

2._____

3._____

4._____

5._____

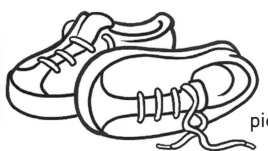

Color in the
pictures on this page.

## Picture How You Can Help

What do you picture when you think of sharing? It's not just giving things. You can do things, too.

Volunteering means doing things to help others.

How?

You could bake cookies, sell them, and give the money to charity.

Have you ever served food at a food bank or holiday dinner? You can help by doing while others are *chewing*!

Have you helped care for pets at a pet shelter?
Do you know how dogs say "thank you?"
A wag of their tail and a lick of their lips!
That says: "Thank you for the treat. It was good to eat!"

There are so many ways for you to give:
Share some money
Give some honey
Bake a cake
For goodness sake!
Give clothes and toys
To other girls and boys.

Sharing is a way of caring. So, if you care, why not share!?

Draw a picture showing how you would like to share.

# SHARING MONEY CROSSWORD PUZZLE

## Clues:

### ACROSS

1. I give to charity because it makes me feel _ _ _ _. (Rhymes with WOOD)

3. Why did Megan share? Because she _ _ _ _ _ (Hint: Rhymes with DARES)

5. Opposite of less: _ _ _ _ (Rhymes with SNORE)

6. When you give to charity, you _ _ _ _ _ _ (Rhymes with NO HATE).

7. Winnie the Pooh likes sharing this sweet treat with his friends: _ _ _ _ _ (Rhymes with FUNNY)

### DOWN

1. Opposite of take: _ _ _ _.

2. Tyler was generous so he _ _ _ _ _ _ with others.

3. A group that helps others is a _ _ _ _ _ _ _ (Rhymes with RARITY).

5. When you share a pizza, you cut a _ _ _ _ _. (Rhymes with MICE)

6. Something you can share, spend, or save: _ _ _ _ _ (Rhymes with HONEY and FUNNY).

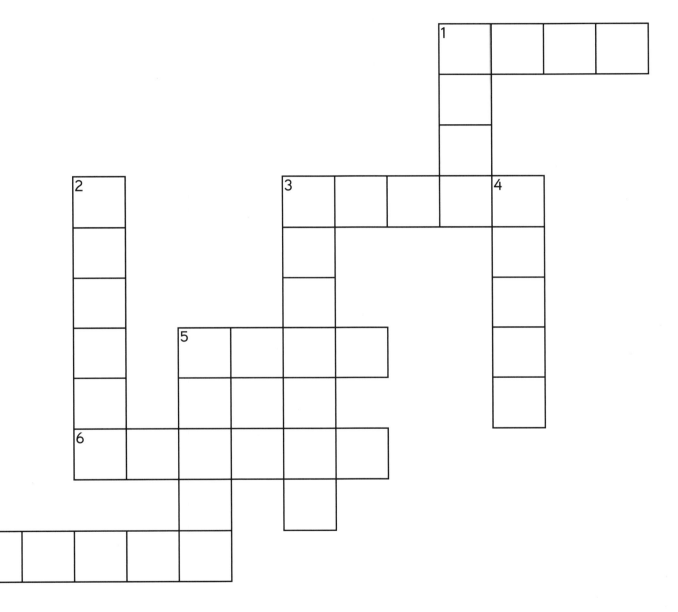

Answers on page 79.

# CHAPTER 8:
# BORROWING MONEY

## Borrowing Money Jumble

1. When you owe money, you have a _ _ _ _.

    T E D B

2. Sally didn't have enough money to pay for her car. So she borrowed some. She took out a _ _ _ _.

    N O L A

3. Sally's loan cost her money. Every month, she needed to pay the bank _ _ _ _ _ _ _ for what she had borrowed.

    I T S T N E R E

4. If you borrow too much money, you might not be able to pay it _ _ _ _.

    A C B K

5. When you pay interest on money that you borrow, you have _ _ _ _ money to spend on other things.

    E S S L

6. When you deposit money in the bank, you _ _ _ _ interest.

R A N E

7. You owe the bank interest when you _ _ _ _ _ _ money.

R O R B O W

8. The bank will let you borrow up to your credit _ _ _ _ _.

I M L I T

Answers on page 79.

# Should You or Should You Not Borrow?

Borrowing money isn't always good. You should only borrow money if you know you can pay it back.

Answer "Y" (YES) or "N" (NO) next to these:

|   | Think about this: Yes or No? | Y | N |
|---|---|---|---|
| 1 | Buy everything you see. |  |  |
| 2 | If you save some money, you could use that to spend. That way you might not need to borrow. |  |  |
| 3 | Be careful not to borrow too much money. |  |  |
| 4 | Pay what you already owe before you borrow more. |  |  |
| 5 | EARNING interest adds to your money. PAYING interest takes away money. |  |  |

Answers on page 79.

# CHAPTER 9:
# SMART MONEY CHOICES

## The Money Adventure Game

Get a dice (a cube with 1 to 6 dots on each side), roll it, move forward the number of spaces rolled, and follow the directions on the board.

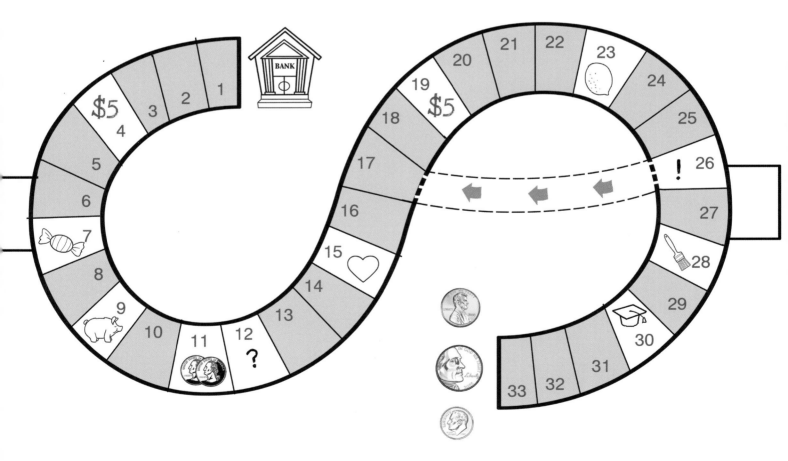

## Rules:

4: You earned $5 walking your neighbor's dog.
 Move up 2 spaces.

7: You spent ALL your allowance on candy.
 Slide down 4 spaces.

9: You saved ALL of your gift money!
 Move ahead 4 spaces.

11: You kept track of all of your money. Good job.
 Move up 2 spaces.

12: You lost all your money and have no clue where it is!
 Slide down to number 5.

15: You gave money to a good charity. Nice!
 Move up 3 spaces.

19: You made a lemonade stand and earned $5. THAT's good business!
 Move up 5 spaces.

23: You shared half of your lemonade earnings with a friend. How generous!
 Move up 4 spaces.

26: You stole someone's money! Oh, no!
 Slide down to number 17.

28: You earned money doing extra chores. Good job!
 Move up 4 spaces.

30: You helped your parents shop and made smart choices. You're a great help!
 Move up 3 spaces.

# NEEDS OR WANTS?

## Do you know your WANTS from your NEEDS?

If you spend all your money
On things you WANT,
You might have none left
For what you NEED.

It may not be
Because of greed.
Sometimes you just
Cannot foresee.

You can buy what you want
If you can still buy what you need.
It's a simple lesson to learn.
So, let's play and take our turn!

We are not all the same
So, there's no one to blame!
And there is no shame
If your answer isn't the same.
Are you ready to play
The Needs or Wants game?

# THE "NEEDS OR WANTS?" GAME

## The Rules:

You have $20 to spend. There's a list of items you could buy. Next to each one, there is a price and two boxes. In the first box, use a pencil to write a W for WANT or an N for NEED. For the second box, write a check mark if you decide to buy it or write an X if not. But first add up the cost of all the NEEDS before you decide what you will buy. Remember, you have $20 in your budget, and you have to buy your NEEDS before you consider your WANTS! This is a good activity to do with an adult.

| Item | Price | Need or Want? | Buy or Not |
|---|---|---|---|
| Sandwich for lunch | $2.00 | | |
| Socks and underwear | $5.00 | | |
| Ice cream | $2.50 | | |
| School supplies: pens, pencils, ruler, notebook | $3.00 | | |
| Movie ticket | $5.00 | | |
| Fancy, cool sneakers (you already have a pair of shoes that are fine) | $50.00 | | |
| Video game | $10.00 | | |
| Cold medicine (you have a bad cold) | $5.00 | | |

As an example, let's say you decided these were needs:
— Sandwich/lunch:       $2.00
— Socks/underwear:      $5.00
— School supplies:       $3.00
—Cold medicine:        $5.00
Total:                   $15.00      $20 - $15 = $5

That means you have $5.00 to spend on wants! Now, go back and see what you can afford for $5.00.

# CAN YOU COMPARE PRICES?

Does your family compare prices when they shop? You can do it too.

Let's look at how much you pay for an ice cream bar.

It costs $2 if you buy it from an ice cream truck. But a box of six ice cream bars at a discount store costs just $3.

If you buy a box of six, how much does each one cost? Divide $3 by 6.

Write your answer here: $3.00 ÷ 6 = _____.
(Hint: It rhymes with "nifty gents"!)

Did you say 50 cents? Correct. Which is a better value? Buy one ice cream bar for $2 or buy 6 for $3 (50¢ each)?

It's your choice: Pay $2 at the ice cream truck and you get one ice cream bar. Or pay $1 more at the discount store, and you get 5 more bars!

*FIVE MORE ICE CREAM BARS!!!!! Yummmm!*

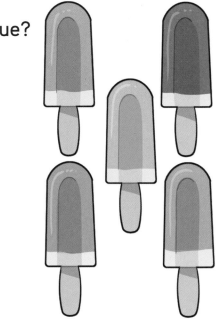

Which would you rather have? Sure, it's hot and you want an ice cream bar now! But if you wait and buy more of them at the discount store, you could buy a few boxes and keep some in the freezer! That way, you will always have some . . . unless an ice cream monster eats them all at once! CHOMP-CHOMP-CHOMP!!!

# CHAPTER 10:
# GROWING MONEY

## Peter and Polly's Contest

Peter and Polly each have $1. They decide to have a contest for one week.

Polly saves her $1 and it doubles every day for the whole week. In just seven days, her money grows a lot.

Peter spends half of his money every day. He saves the rest and it doubles every day. How much will he have after seven days? Let's find out.

| Date | Each day Polly starts with: | It doubles to |
|---|---|---|
| Sept 1 | $1 | $2 |
| Sept 2 | $2 | $4 |
| Sept 3 | $4 | $8 |
| Sept 4 | $8 | $16 |
| Sept 5 | $16 | $32 |
| Sept 6 | $32 | $64 |
| Sept 7 | $64 | $128 |

What happens to Peter's money? He spends half of it each day. The other half of his money he saves and it doubles:

Day 1: $1 – 50¢ spent = 50¢ saved x 2 = $1
Day 2: $1 – 50¢ spent = 50¢ saved x 2 = $1
Day 3: $1 – 50¢ spent = 50¢ saved x 2 = $1
Day 4: $1 – 50¢ spent = 50¢ saved x 2 = $1

You see the pattern. Every day Peter ends up with what he started with. His money never grows. After 7 days he still has $1 and Polly has $128.

In real life, money can grow by earning interest. It will grow more slowly than in this example. But over time, it can grow and grow. And it will grow even more if you add to it by saving money each month.

# HOW MUCH CAN MONEY GROW?

If you save $5 every month, how much would you have after one year?

    A) $50

    B) $60

    C) $75

Multiply $5 x 12 or count by fives.

| | | | |
|---|---|---|---|
| January<br>$5 | +February<br>$5 | +March<br>$5 | +April<br>$5 |
| +May<br>$5 | +June<br>$5 | +July<br>$5 | +August<br>$5 |
| +September<br>$5 | +October<br>$5 | +November<br>$5 | +December<br>$5 |

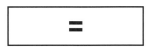

Answers on page 79.

# HOW MUCH CAN MONEY GROW WITH INTEREST?

When you deposit money in the bank, it earns interest. That means your money can earn you MORE money!

If you save $5 each month and earn $1 interest each month, how much money would you have after one year?

A) $61
B) $70
C) $72

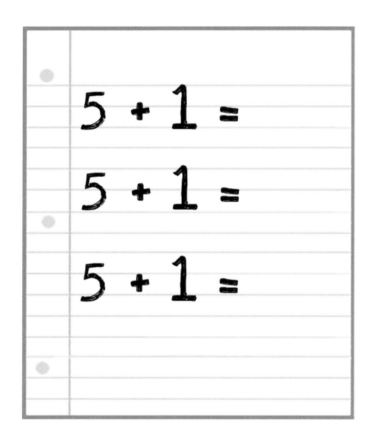

Answers on page 79.

## Money Lessons

Money:
Earn it. Use it.
Spend it. Share it.
Save it. Buy it.
Want to try it?

Take your money. Treat it well.
Save-spend-share. Time will tell if you do it well.
Live without stuff if you can't afford it.
Save some now and you'll be rewarded!

Money is good but use it well
And over time you will tell:
You can have just what you need
But be careful not to fall into greed!

I hope you liked this book about money.
I tried to keep it light and a little bit funny.
But most of all, I wanted to teach
That being good with money is within your reach!


Thank you,


Allan Kunigis

# ANSWERS

**Pages 9-10**
How Much Are These Coins
Worth?
Penny, 1¢
Nickel, 5¢
Dime, 10¢
Quarter, 25¢

**Page 11**
Coin Matching Game
Penny = 1¢
Nickel = 5¢
Dime = 10¢
Quarter = 25¢
Dollar = 100¢

**Page 18**
Buying a 10¢ pickle: 1 dime or
2 nickels or 10 pennies

Feeding your bunny: You can
buy 4 carrots with 4 quarters

**Page 20**
Buying a 10¢ eraser: 1 dime, 2
nickels, or 10 pennies
Paying with a quarter, you
would get 15¢ change.

**Page 21**
Buying a 49¢ notebook: 1
quarter, 2 dimes, zero nickels,
and 4 pennies = 49¢.

**Page 22**
Buying a 97¢ box of crayons: 3
quarters, 2 dimes, zero nickels,
and 2 pennies = 97¢.

**Page 13**
Crossword Puzzle

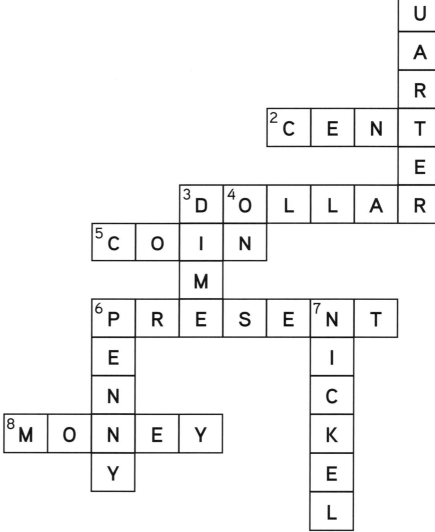

## Page 23
### Coin Maze

## Page 25
### Connect the Dots

## Page 27
### Crossword Puzzle

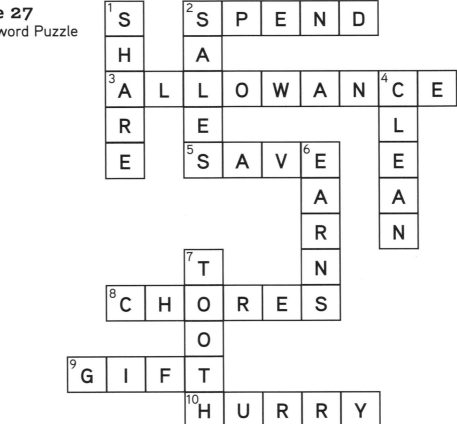

## Page 29
Bake Sale: Lucas earned $6, Sophia earned $10, Emily earned $12. Together, they earned $28.

## Page 33-34
Money Jumble
1. Free
2. Bank
3. Gold
4. Deal
5. Sale
6. Save
7. Money
8. Share

## Page 35-36
Money Rhymes
1. Brave Dave: SAVE
2. Claire's Bear: SHARE
3. Jen's Friend: SPEND
4. Roy Joy: TOY
5. Benny Any: PENNY
6. Hopped Flopped Bopped: SHOP

## Page 39
Show Me the Money Word Search

## Page 42
Secret Code answer: SAVE SOME MONEY

## Page 43
Unscrambled answer: DON'T SPEND ALL YOUR MONEY

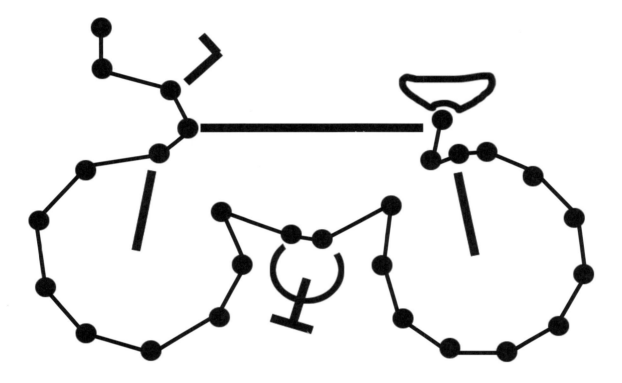

## Page 45
What would you save for? In the example, it would take 10 months of saving $10 each month to reach $100 in savings.

## Page 46
Secret Code answers:
Banks keep your money SAFE.
In a bank, your money can earn INTEREST.
Putting money in your bank account is a DEPOSIT.

**Page 51**
Crossword Puzzle

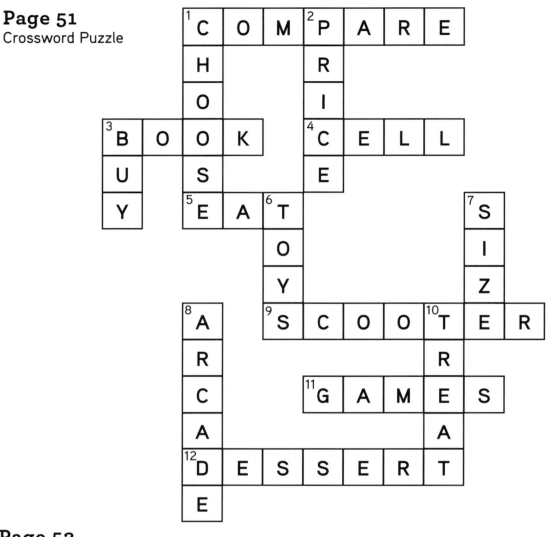

**Page 52**
Match the Coupons

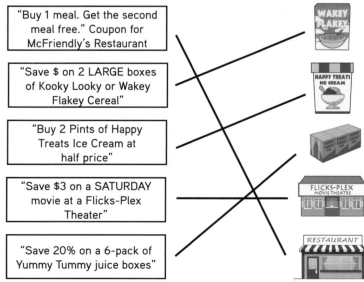

"Buy 1 meal. Get the second meal free." Coupon for McFriendly's Restaurant

"Save $ on 2 LARGE boxes of Kooky Looky or Wakey Flakey Cereal"

"Buy 2 Pints of Happy Treats Ice Cream at half price"

"Save $3 on a SATURDAY movie at a Flicks-Plex Theater"

"Save 20% on a 6-pack of Yummy Tummy juice boxes"

**Page 59**
Crossword Puzzle

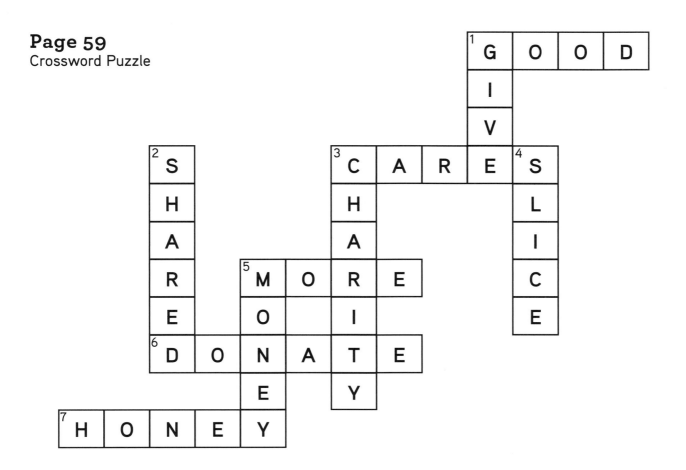

**Page 60-61**
Borrowing Money Jumble

1. Debt
2. Loan
3. Interest
4. Back
5. Less
6. Earn
7. Borrow
8. Limit

**Page 62**
Should You or Should You Not Borrow?
1. No
2. Yes
3. Yes
4. Yes
5. Yes

**Page 71**
How much can money grow?

B) $60. $5 saved every month for 12 months adds up to $60.

**Page 72**
How much can money grow with interest?

C) $72. $5 saved every month for 12 months plus $1 interest each month adds up to $72.